AMICUS LEARNING

NOODLE-MANIA

A Cookbook for Kids Who Love PASTA

by Teresa Klepinger

AMICUS HIGH INTEREST is published by
Amicus Learning, an imprint of Amicus
P.O. Box 227, Mankato, MN 56002
www.amicuspublishing.us

LIBRARY OF CONGRESS CATALOGING-IN-PUBLICATION DATA
Names: Klepinger, Teresa author
Title: Noodlemania : a cookbook for kids who love pasta / by: Teresa Klepinger.
Description: Mankato, Minnesota : Amicus Learning, [2026] | Series: Kids in the kitchen | Audience: Ages
7–10 | Audience: Grades 4–6 | Summary: "Simple pasta recipes for tweens and teens inspire kids to
experiment in the kitchen. This cookbook features easy-to-follow recipes, step-by-step instructions,
safety tips, a glossary, and party-hosting tips. Perfect for budding chefs to explore pasta and
experiment with flavors!"– Provided by publisher.
Identifiers: LCCN 2025021478 (print) | LCCN 2025021479 (ebook) | ISBN 9798892008716 library binding |
ISBN 9798892009379 paperback | ISBN 9798896850038 ebook
Subjects: LCSH: Cooking–Juvenile literature | Cooking (Pasta) –Juvenile literature | Pasta products–
Juvenile literature | LCGFT: Cookbooks
Classification: LCC TX652.5 .K586 2026 (print) | LCC TX652.5 (ebook) | DDC 641.82/2–dc23/eng/20250702
LC record available at https://lccn.loc.gov/2025021478
LC ebook record available at https://lccn.loc.gov/2025021479

PHOTO CREDITS: Adobe Stock/Brent Hofacker, 13; Amicus/Kim Pfeffer, 7; Freepik/baitelman, cover,
1; Getty Images/LauriPatterson, 27; Shutterstock/alex mino10, 23, artem evdokimov, 22 (bottom), Brent
Hofacker, 10, 30, DronG, 15, Erhan Inga, 8, Foodio, 18, gowithstock, 14 (middle), grey_and, 4, Igor
Normann, 21, JPL Designs, 24, Katarzyna Hurova, 5, Koko Foto, 28, Marie C Fields, 17, Max Acronym, 26,
Nataly Studio, 12, New Africa, 22 (top), pedphoto36pm, 14 (top), soeka, 22 (middle), studiovin, 11, Tanya
Consaul Photography, 20, Tatjana Baibakova, 25, The Image Party, 14 (bottom), Timolina, 28

EDITOR: Rebecca Glaser
SERIES DESIGNER: Kim Pfeffer
BOOK DESIGNER: Emily Dietz

Printed in the United States of America

—•— CONTENTS —•—

4

PASTA PERFECTION

6

BEFORE YOU START

8

RECIPES

32

HOST A PASTA DINNER PARTY!

PASTA
PERFECTION

PASTA, noodles, macaroni - whatever you call it - people love it! You probably have a favorite family recipe. Pasta can be a creamy comfort food, a warm soup for a cold night, or a yummy salad for a festive get-together. Now you can learn to cook it yourself! It's super easy to prepare—just boil it in water.

Pasta comes in more than 350 different shapes, which makes this favorite food not only delicious, but fun! Whether your favorite shape is a long noodle, a corkscrew, bow tie, or wagon wheel, in this cookbook you'll find a delicious recipe for it. Best of all, with you as the cook, you can add (or subtract) the ingredients you want and turn your dish into absolute perfection. Let's get started!

COOKING GLOSSARY

BEAT   To stir rapidly with a whisk or electric mixer to add air.

BLEND   To gently combine dry ingredients to make a smooth mixture.

BOIL   To heat a liquid until bubbles form and break at the surface or to cook in boiling water.

MIX   To stir until the ingredients are combined well, often combining liquids and dry ingredients.

SIMMER   To cook slowly in a liquid just below the boiling point.

STIR   To use a spoon to loosely combine ingredients.

WHISK   To stir with a tool made with loops of wire, also called a whisk. Use a fork if you don't have a whisk.

METRIC CONVERSION CHART

1 teaspoon (tsp.) = 5 ml	1 cup = 240 ml
1 tablespoon (Tbsp.) = 15 ml	1 quart = 1 liter
¼ cup = 60 ml	1 pound = 453 g
⅓ cup = 80 ml	1 ounce (oz.) = 28 g
½ cup = 120 ml	16 oz. = 460 g

GETTING READY

 Wash your hands.

 Wear an apron to protect your clothes.

 Tie back loose hair.

 Read the whole recipe first.

 Gather all your ingredients before you start.

 Ask for an adult's help if you're not sure how to do something.

HELPFUL TIPS

- Use a **LARGE POT** of water to cook pasta. It needs room to move around as it boils. **STIR** the pasta into the water and while it cooks to keep it from sticking to the bottom.

- Add **SALT** to the water, about 1 or 2 tsp., to improve the flavor. Always start with a small amount!

- Once you **DRAIN** the pasta, it will get sticky quickly. If it needs to sit for a few minutes before you put the sauce on, rinse it with cold water.

HOMEMADE NOODLES

With homemade pasta, you can make any shape you want! How about lightning bolts? Or flowers? You can even spell your name!

SERVINGS: 2-3

TIME:

- 1½ hours (including 45 minutes of rest time for the dough)

INGREDIENTS

- 1 cup flour
- ½ tsp. salt
- 1 egg, beaten
- 1 tsp. olive oil
- 3-6 tsp. water

EQUIPMENT

- Medium mixing bowl
- Spoon
- Measuring cups and spoons
- Plastic wrap
- Rolling pin
- Pizza cutter
- Large pot
- Colander

— • — STEPS — • —

1. **MAKE DOUGH.** Blend the flour and salt in the bowl. Make a well in the middle of the flour and pour in the beaten egg and olive oil. Stir the flour into the egg gradually. Switch to using your hands once it starts to come together. Add water 1 tsp. at a time if you can't get all the flour into the dough ball.

2. **KNEAD.** Dust a smooth surface with a pinch of flour. Set the dough ball on it and knead it. Kneading means pushing down on the dough with the heel of your hands, turning and folding the dough over, then pressing, turning, and folding again. Do this over and over for 5 minutes. (Set a timer.) The dough will get smooth and flexible.

3. **REST.** Wrap the dough in plastic wrap. Let it rest on the counter for at least 45 minutes. This lets the dough "relax" so you can roll it out.

4. **ROLL.** Shape the dough into an oval. Press the rolling pin into the center and roll toward the ends of the dough. Use some muscle. Keep rolling until the dough is about 1/16 inch (1.5 mm) thick. Be patient.

5. **SLICE.** Use the pizza cutter to slice the dough into spaghetti-sized strips, or create other shapes with small cookie cutters.

6. **COOK.** Bring a pot of salted water to boil. Add the noodles and cook for 4 minutes. Test a noodle. If it is chewy or tastes raw, cook for 1 more minute at a time until they are tender. (Thicker, wider noodles take longer to cook.) Drain and serve with your favorite sauce!

RECIPE 2

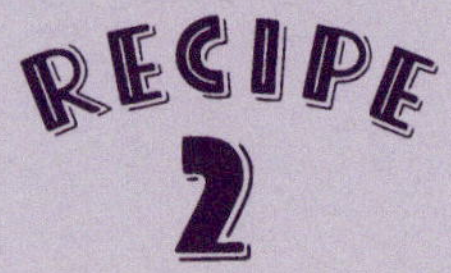

ANGEL HAIR PASTA WITH PARMESAN

A delicious lunch that can be ready in about the time it takes to make a sandwich!

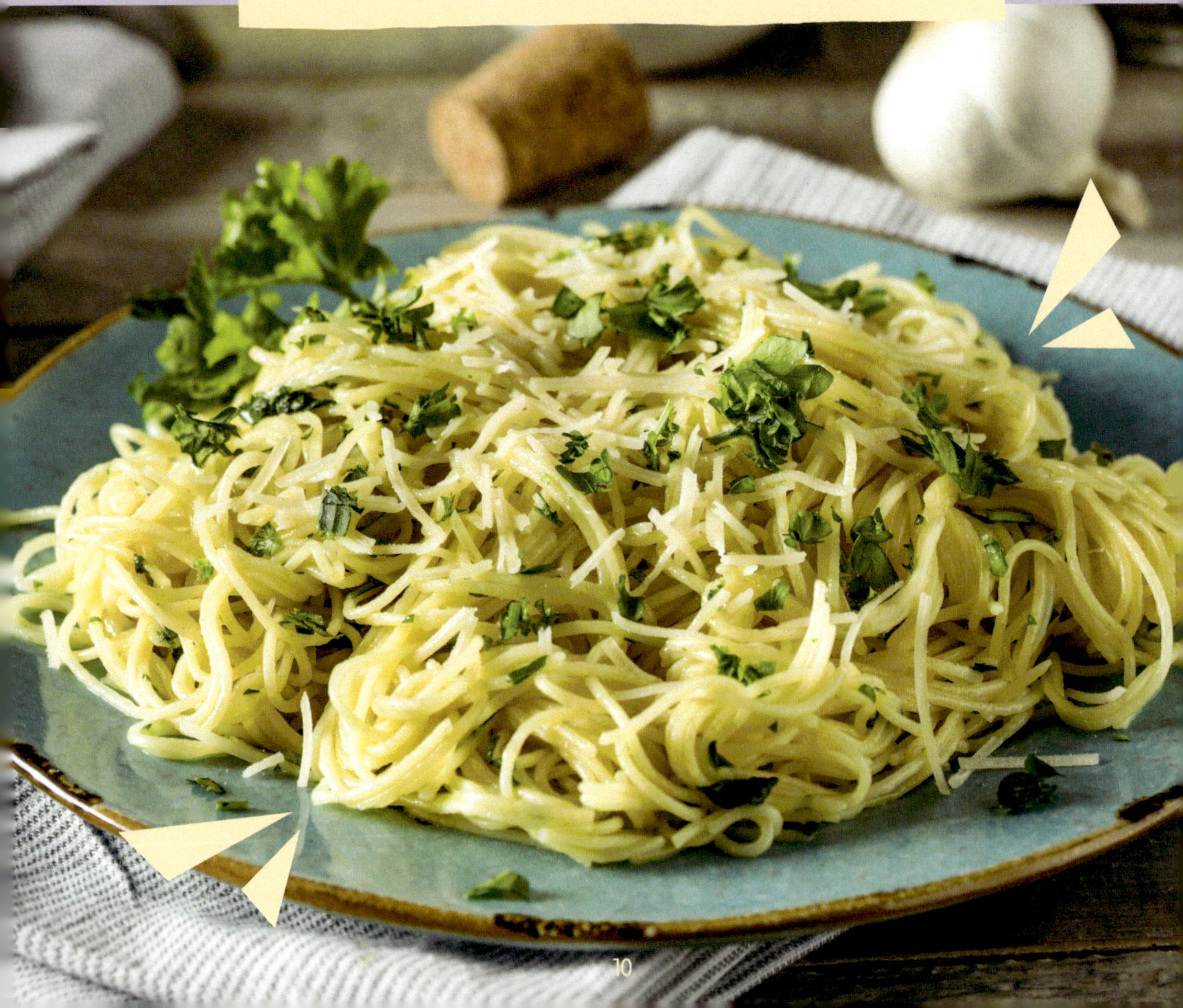

SERVINGS: 4

TIME:

- 20 minutes plus cooling time

INGREDIENTS

- 1 pound angel hair pasta
- 1–2 tsp. salt
- ¼ cup olive oil
- 4 cloves garlic
- ½–¾ cup grated Parmesan cheese
- Optional: A squeeze of lemon, chopped parsley, a shake of Italian seasoning

EQUIPMENT

- Large pot
- Pasta spoon
- Colander
- Large skillet
- Cutting board
- Kitchen knife
- Measuring cups and spoons
- Spatula or wooden spoon

STEPS

1. **BOIL.** Set a pot of water on the stove to boil, then cook the pasta according to the directions on the package.

2. **CHOP.** While you wait for the water to boil, peel and finely chop the garlic.

3. **COOK.** Heat the oil in the skillet to medium and cook the garlic until it smells great, 1 to 2 minutes. Remove the pan from the heat if the pasta isn't ready yet.

4. **STIR TOGETHER.** Drain the pasta and pour it into the skillet. Stir it quickly until the noodles are coated with the oil and garlic. Add a little bit more oil if it looks too dry. (Or add 1 Tbsp. butter. Yum.)

5. **ADD CHEESE.** Sprinkle the grated cheese on top and keep stirring until it begins to melt.

6. **SERVE.** Serve immediately with salt and pepper.

RECIPE 3

MACARONI AND CHEESE

SERVINGS: 4

TIME:

- 30 minutes

EQUIPMENT

- Large pot
- Pasta spoon
- Colander
- Large mixing spoon
- Whisk
- Measuring cups and spoons
- Cheese grater
- Small mixing bowl

INGREDIENTS

- ½ pound elbow macaroni (2 cups)
- 1½ tsp. salt
- 4 Tbsp. butter
- 2 eggs
- 1 can (12 oz.) evaporated milk, heated to warm, divided
- 1 Tbsp. yellow mustard
- 3 cups grated cheddar cheese

STEPS

1. **START MACARONI.** Set a pot of water to boil and cook the macaroni according to the directions on the box, but for 1 minute less than it says.

2. **WHISK AND GRATE.** Meanwhile, whisk the eggs, 1 cup (8 oz.) of evaporated milk, and the mustard in the mixing bowl. Grate the cheese.

3. **DRAIN.** When the macaroni is cooked, drain it in the colander. Return the macaroni to the pot.

4. **MELT BUTTER.** Turn the heat to medium-low and add the butter to the macaroni. Stir until the butter is melted.

5. **ADD INGREDIENTS.** Add the milk mixture and 2 cups of the cheese. Stir constantly until the cheese starts to melt. Slowly add the rest of the evaporated milk and cheese.

6. **STIR.** Stir constantly until the sauce is thick and smooth and hot, about 5 minutes. Serve immediately.

PICK YOUR PASTA

In any of these recipes, you can switch out the pasta shape. Don't have macaroni? Use wagon wheels or bow tie pasta. They taste the same.

HOT DOG MACARONI

Cook hot dogs and slice. Mix into macaroni and cheese when your sauce is almost done.

WHITE CHEDDAR MACARONI

Follow the recipe on pg 12 and substitute white cheddar for regular cheddar.

PIZZA MACARONI

Cook pasta, drain, and mix with pizza sauce. Melt mozzarella on the top.

CHEESEBURGER MACARONI
Cook ground beef in a skillet until it's fully browned. Mix into your macaroni and cheese when the sauce is almost done.

CHICKEN NOODLE SOUP

This is the REAL thing, made fresh! It tastes WAY better than heating up a can of mushy soup.

SERVINGS: 4–6

TIME:

- 30 minutes

EQUIPMENT

- Large pot
- Kitchen knife
- Cutting board
- Long-handled spoon
- Nylon or rubber spatula
- Measuring cups and spoons

INGREDIENTS

- 1 Tbsp. cooking oil
- 6–8 chicken tenderloins
- 1 quart chicken broth (4 cups)
- ½ cup onion, chopped
- 1 celery stalk, chopped
- 1 bay leaf (optional)
- ¼ tsp. dried thyme leaves
- 1 cup frozen peas and carrots
- ½ cup frozen corn
- 2 cups egg noodles

STEPS

1. **COOK.** Heat 1 Tbsp. of oil in the pot on medium heat. Add the onions, celery, and chicken. Cook and stir with the nylon spatula for 5–7 minutes on each side or until the chicken is no longer pink in the middle. Remove the chicken to a cutting board (leave the vegetables) and allow to cool.

2. **ADD BROTH AND HERBS.** Add the chicken broth, bay leaf, and thyme to the pot. Bring it to a boil. While you're waiting, tear or cut the chicken into small bite-size pieces.

3. **ADD VEGETABLES.** Add the peas, carrots, and corn to the pot. Bring it back to a boil. Lower the heat and let it simmer for 5 minutes.

4. **ADD NOODLES.** Turn the heat back up to medium high and add the noodles. Once it boils, lower the heat so it stays at a low boil for 9 minutes.

5. **ADD CHICKEN.** Add the chicken to the pot. Turn off the heat.

6. **LET SIT.** Let the flavors mix for 5 more minutes. Serve warm!

YOU'RE THE COOK!

In any recipe, if you don't like a particular ingredient, like onions or celery, just leave it out. Or add more of what you love. It's okay to make it the way you want it!

SPAGHETTI AND MARINARA

The classic! Now you can make it fresh with YOUR favorite touches!

SERVINGS: 8

TIME:

- 40 minutes

EQUIPMENT

- Large pot
- Deep frying pan or large pot for cooking the sauce
- Pasta spoon
- Colander
- Kitchen knife
- Cutting board
- Flexible spatula
- Measuring spoons
- Can opener

- 1 pound spaghetti
- 2 15-oz. cans tomato sauce
- 1 6-oz. can tomato paste
- ½ cup chopped onion (optional)
- 2 cloves chopped or pressed garlic
- 2 Tbsp. olive oil
- 2 tsp. Italian seasoning
- 1 cup grated Parmesan cheese
- 1 tsp. sugar (optional)
- 1 pound ground beef, cooked (optional)
- 8 oz. sliced veggies (optional)
- Salt and pepper

STEPS

1. **CHOP AND COOK.** Chop the onion and garlic. Heat the oil in a deep frying pan or pot on medium. Add the chopped onion and garlic. Cook and stir until it is soft and smells good, about 5 minutes. Don't let the garlic brown or it will be bitter.

2. **ADD INGREDIENTS.** Add tomato sauce, tomato paste, and Italian seasoning. Stir together. If you want options like ground beef or sliced veggies, add those too.

3. **COOK SPAGHETTI.** Set a large pot of water to boil and cook the spaghetti according to the directions. If you didn't buy already grated Parmesan cheese, grate it now.

4. **SIMMER THE SAUCE.** While the spaghetti is cooking, keep stirring the sauce until it starts to bubble. Let it simmer for at least 10 minutes. If you have time, give it about 30 minutes to let the flavors blend together. Taste it and add sugar if you think it needs it, and more seasoning if you want a stronger flavor.

5. **DRAIN.** Drain the spaghetti and dish it onto dinner plates.

6. **SERVE.** Spoon the sauce onto the noodles and sprinkle with Parmesan cheese.

FETTUCCINE ALFREDO

Rich, creamy, and so delicious! It's hard to find someone who doesn't love it!

INGREDIENTS

- 1 pound fettuccine noodles
- 2 cups freshly grated Parmesan (Get a wedge of Parmesan. Pre-grated Parmesan won't melt properly.)
- 6 Tbsp. butter
- 1 cup heavy cream or half-and-half
- ½ tsp. garlic salt
- Pepper to taste

EQUIPMENT

- Large pot
- Medium pot
- Cheese grater
- Colander
- Pasta spoon
- Measuring cups and spoons

STEPS

1. **COOK PASTA.** Set a pot of water to boil and cook the fettuccine according to the package directions.

2. **COMBINE.** While the noodles are cooking, melt the butter with the cream on low heat in a medium to large saucepan or pot. Stir the sauce frequently.

3. **SEASON.** Add pepper and garlic salt to the cream mixture.

4. **SLOWLY ADD CHEESE.** When the sauce is barely simmering, add the grated cheese a little at a time, stirring until it is all melted together. Don't let it boil or the sauce might separate, which means the butter, cream, and cheese won't mix properly. Keep it warm while the noodles finish cooking.

5. **DRAIN NOODLES.** Drain the noodles into a colander. Then put them back in the pot.

6. **STIR TOGETHER.** Pour the cheese sauce over the noodles. Stir it all together until the noodles are coated. Enjoy!

Fettucine alfredo tastes great with other ingredients. Once you've mastered the basic recipe, try these variations.

CHICKEN BROCCOLI

Cut up chicken pieces. Heat oil in a skillet and fry. Cook broccoli in a microwave. Mix cooked chicken and broccoli into the alfredo sauce and cook about 2 minutes more.

MUSHROOM

In a skillet, heat 1 tsp. of olive oil and lightly cook mushrooms. Add a bit of salt and pepper to taste. Mix into alfredo sauce when it's almost done and cook about 2 minutes more.

SHRIMP

Rinse shrimp under water and pat dry with paper towels. Cook in a skillet with 1 tsp. olive oil until shrimp turns white. Mix into alfredo sauce when it's almost done and cook about 2 minutes more.

FOUR CHEESE

Use ¼ cup each of grated Parmesan, Romano, mozarella, and fontina cheeses. Combine for a flavorful alfredo sauce.

RICE NOODLES WITH PEANUT SAUCE

Start with delicious noodles and sauce, then add veggies and chicken for a one-pot dinner!

SERVINGS: 4

TIME:

- 40 minutes

EQUIPMENT

- Large skillet
- Large pot
- Colander
- Pasta spoon
- Medium mixing bowl
- Measuring cups and spoons

INGREDIENTS

- 1 pound chicken tenderloins
- 200 grams rice noodles (or half of a 14-oz. package)
- 3-4 cups chopped vegetables (carrots, broccoli, snow peas, etc.)
- 1-4 Tbsp. water
- 1 lime cut into 4 wedges

SAUCE INGREDIENTS

- ½ cup peanut butter
- ¼ cup soy sauce
- ¼ cup brown sugar
- ¼ cup rice vinegar
- 1 tsp. garlic powder
- 1 Tbsp. sesame oil (optional)

STEPS

1. **COOK NOODLES.** Set a pot of water to boil and cook the rice noodles according to the package directions. Test a noodle for tenderness before draining. Cook for an additional 1 minute at a time until they're done. Drain and rinse them under cold water.

2. **COOK CHICKEN AND VEGETABLES.** While the noodles cook, place the chicken and vegetables in the skillet. Fill with water to cover the chicken. Bring to boil over high heat, then turn down to medium-low and simmer for 6-8 minutes or until chicken is no longer pink in the middle.

3. **DRAIN AND SHRED.** Drain the water. Remove the chicken to a cutting board. When it is cool enough to handle, shred it into bite-size pieces, with a knife and fork or your hands. Then return it to the skillet.

4. **MAKE SAUCE.** Add the peanut sauce ingredients to the medium bowl. Stir with a whisk until well blended. Add 1 Tbsp. of water at a time if it seems too thick.

5. **MIX.** Pour the noodles into the skillet with the chicken and vegetables. Pour the sauce over it all and mix over low heat until everything is coated and the food is hot.

6. **SERVE.** Serve with a lime wedge to squeeze over the dish.

CORKSCREW PASTA SALAD

Store this yummy salad in the fridge and have it for lunch or a snack. It's great on a hot summer day.

SERVINGS: 6

TIME:

- 30–45 minutes

EQUIPMENT

- Large pot
- Colander
- Pasta spoon
- Large bowl for serving
- Medium mixing bowl
- Whisk
- Kitchen knife
- Cutting board
- Measuring cups and spoons
- Mixing spoon

INGREDIENTS

- ¼ cup milk
- ¾ cup sour cream
- ¾ cup mayonnaise
- 1 packet powdered Italian salad dressing
- 4 cups corkscrew (or rotini) pasta (usually ¾ of a 1-pound package)
- ¼ pound sliced Genoa salami
- 1½ cup frozen peas, thawed
- 4 ounces sliced black olives (small can)
- Other veggies (optional):
  - ½ cup chopped celery
  - 2 sliced green onions, including the green tops
  - Chopped bell pepper (any color)
  - Cherry tomatoes, cut in half
  - Broccoli pieces
- Salt and pepper to taste

STEPS

1. **MIX DRESSING.** Make the dressing by mixing the milk, mayonnaise, sour cream, and Italian salad dressing powder in a medium bowl. Whisk together until it's smooth. Place in the refrigerator.

2. **COOK PASTA.** Set a pot of water to boil and cook the pasta according to the package directions. Drain in the colander and rinse with cold water.

3. **PREPARE VEGGIES.** While you're waiting for the pasta to cook, thaw the peas. Slice the salami into cubes. Drain the olives. Chop any other vegetables you want to add.

4. **COMBINE.** Pour the pasta into the large serving bowl. Add the peas, salami, olives, and other vegetables.

5. **STIR.** Pour the dressing on top and stir until it is well mixed. Add salt and pepper to taste.

6. **CHILL AND SERVE.** You can serve immediately, but if you have time, chill for 30 to 60 minutes in the refrigerator to let the flavors blend.

RECIPE 9

BAKED FETA PASTA

This recipe was also called "TikTok Pasta" because from 2021 to 2025, it was the most viral TikTok recipe of all time.

SERVINGS: 4

TIME:

- 10 minutes (prep)
- 40 minutes (bake)

INGREDIENTS

- 2 pints cherry or grape tomatoes
- ½ cup olive oil
- Salt and pepper to taste
- 1 block (8 oz.) feta cheese
- 1 pound penne or bow tie pasta
- ½ tsp. salt
- 4 cloves chopped garlic
- 1 tsp. dried basil, or ¼ cup chopped fresh basil

EQUIPMENT

- Large pot
- Colander
- Pasta spoon
- 9 x 13-inch (23 x 33-cm) baking dish
- Large stirring spoon
- Measuring cups and spoons
- Kitchen knife
- Cutting board
- Square baking pan

STEPS

1. **PREP.** Preheat oven to 400°F (200°C). Wash cherry tomatoes and place them in the baking dish. Drizzle with olive oil and stir until the tomatoes are coated. Sprinkle with salt and pepper.

2. **ADD CHEESE.** Place the block of cheese in the middle of the tomatoes and drizzle a little more olive oil on top of it.

3. **BAKE AND BOIL.** Bake for 40 minutes. After 20 minutes, start to cook the pasta according to the instructions on the package so it will be ready when the tomatoes are done. When the tomatoes are done baking, they will be wrinkly and browned.

4. **MIX AND MASH.** Add the chopped garlic and basil to the tomatoes and stir it all together, mashing the tomatoes as you go.

5. **COMBINE.** Drain the pasta, reserving ½ cup of the pasta water. Dump the pasta into the tomatoes and stir again. If it looks a little too dry, add the reserved water.

6. **STIR.** Stir the whole thing again. Check to see if it needs more salt and pepper, and serve!

LASAGNA CASSEROLE

Regular lasagna is tricky to make. This yummy version tastes just like lasagna but is super easy!

SERVINGS: 6–8

TIME:

• 1 hour

EQUIPMENT

• Nonstick cooking spray
• Large pot
• Deep skillet or large pot for cooking the sauce
• Pasta spoon
• Colander
• Kitchen knife
• Cutting board
• Flexible spatula
• Medium sized mixing bowl
• Mixing spoon
• Measuring cups and spoons
• 9 x 13-inch (23 x 33-cm) baking dish

- 1 pound penne pasta
- 1 pound ground beef
- 1 Tbsp. salt
- ½ tsp. garlic powder
- 1 tsp. Italian seasoning
- ½ cup chopped onion (optional)
- 1 egg
- 1 15-oz. container ricotta cheese
- 2 cups shredded mozzarella cheese (8-oz. package)
- ½ cup shredded Parmesan cheese
- 1 jar (24 oz.) marinara sauce, or use recipe on p. 19

STEPS

1. **PREP AND BOIL PASTA.** Preheat the oven to 350°F (180°C). Set a pot of water to boil and cook the pasta according to the package directions, BUT for 1–2 minutes less than it says. Drain pasta into the colander.

2. **COOK.** While pasta boils, cook the chopped onion and ground beef over medium-high heat. Break the meat into small pieces as you go. When the meat is no longer pink, drain the grease.

3. **ADD INGREDIENTS.** Add the garlic powder and Italian seasoning to the meat. Pour in the marinara sauce. Turn the heat down to medium and stir until sauce is well-blended. Allow it to simmer for 1–2 minutes.

4. **MAKE CHEESE MIXTURE.** Empty the ricotta cheese into the mixing bowl. Add the egg and stir until blended. Save a little cheese for topping. Add the rest of the mozzarella cheese and Parmesan cheese to the mixture and stir.

5. **MIX AND POUR.** In a large pot, mix the noodles, meat mixture, and cheese mixture together. Spray your baking dish with nonstick spray. Pour everything into the baking dish.

6. **BAKE.** Cover the dish with foil and bake for 30 minutes. Remove the foil. Sprinkle the rest of the cheese on top and bake for 5 minutes more. Take it out of the oven and let it sit for 5 minutes. Then serve!

HOST A PASTA DINNER PARTY!

Show off what you learned about cooking **PASTA** by having some friends over for dinner! Here are a few ideas and tips to make your event extra special.

- **GUEST LIST/FOOD ALLERGIES:** Invite your friends and check to see if someone needs a gluten-free or dairy-free option. Make sure everyone has something safe to eat.

- **SET UP & PRESENTATION:** It's fun to decorate Italian! How about a red and white checked tablecloth and green, red, and white plates and napkins? Be creative!

- **FOOD:** Prepare three separate pasta shapes. Then have three sauces—maybe alfredo, marinara, and marinara with ground beef added. Then your guests can mix and match on their plates! Serve with extra grated Parmesan, Italian bread, and a green salad.

- **BE A GOOD HOST:** Play music in the background. Refill drinks as needed and offer seconds. Pass the bread!

- **CLEAN UP:** When everyone is done eating, ask them to help clean up. Toss the trash in a bag, refrigerate leftovers, and load dishes in the dishwasher. It's quick and easy when you do it together!

With these tasty tips, your pasta party will be saucy, satisfying, and full of fun!